OPERA

To Ariel / with best wishes / [signature] / 8-Feb-2004

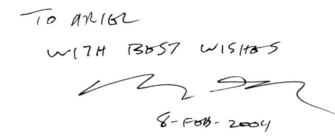

OPERA
POEMS 1981-2002

Barry Schwabsky

Meritage Press
San Francisco & St. Helena

Acknowledgements:
Some of these poems have been previously published in the magazines *Artforum, Bad Henry Review, Monkey Puzzle, Mudfish, N.A.P. Text(s), o-blek, Pierogi Press*, and *Spazio Umano/Human Space* as well as in the anthology *E.S.P.* (Dooley de Cappelaine Gallery).

"Hidden Figure" was published by Collectif Générations (Colombes, France) as the text for a limited-edition artist's book with collages by Jessica Stockholder.

"Drafts (of Water)" was published (under the title "Drafts of Water") by Edizioni Canopo (Prato, Italy) as the text for a limited-edition artist's book with prints by Luisa Rabbia.

Meritage Press books are published by Eileen Tabios who thanks "Oenophiles For Poetry" for their support.

Book design by Sandy McIntosh.
Meritage Press logo by Theresa Chong.

ISBN No. 0970917929

Meritage Press
2275 Broadway, Suite 312
San Francisco, CA 94115
www.MeritagePress.com
MeritagePress@aol.com

Contents

I

Opera

It happened. A kiss
pressed on unwilling lips
explained, "Be
mine, be faithful
anticipation
of those harsher seasons
downstream." Downstream,
our boat rocked on algebraic waves.
The poet who thinks for me
detests the writer who bears my name.
He would like to compose
the luxury editions he
can't afford to buy. And he plays
the scold and writes this down
in ruled notebooks.
A ghostly figure beckons
through waking mist:
"I love my bed of grass
as well as sky, the all-
containing." He said
my bouquet's all burnt
only yes it isn't.

*

Downstream echoes the psalm
you strained to hear,
the kiss you pressed
on unwilling lips
more willing now to blame resistance
in this bed of grass

and shrewd fear. The meadow
blew in waves. You've singed
the little white flowers,
their edges turn
brittlest smoke. We
who read with our pens
invent beautiful reasons.
You the thief of what can't
be stolen are their faithful
servant. Here I dine without salt
of memory or consolation,
true Adamic labor.

*

Corrected hair. Face smooth
as mirror. Unsurpassable song.
Living death. Unhanded. Unhanded.
Theatrical weeping. "He" becomes "she"
and "you" becomes "he" and "we"
becomes "we" becomes "we" becomes "we."
Pears shaped like apples. Pears
that taste like apples that taste like grapes.

*

Pleasure is the new pain.
The voice in the mirror
extorts the most willing
kisses. Are they softer
than you are? There are more
and they are yours
and they soften with time

along with all my best mistakes.
I hereby unrecognize you,
sweet study of limit.

Opera (Karen O sings the remastered military bandwidth mix)

We have complete mastery
of the air.

        The air between
one mouth and another
may be mastered in the name
of a kiss.

        Equinox will mark
the extreme season. Enter this
in ruled notebooks.

        A ghostly figure,
the all-containing, extends a burnt bouquet

through mists of limit.

*

We have complete mastery
of the air.

        The breath between
unjust mouths offers no resistance
on the world stage.

        We've forgotten
our shrewd fears. Divine plan:
to burn the little white flowers.

We
who read with our pens invent
divine unreason.

The road to peace
is correcting the adversary's hair.

Fear tastes like apples.

Tears taste like grapes.

*

We have complete mastery
of the air.

Democracy spreads
with explosive kisses. They water
our grass, the all-containing.

Our grass,
what can never be stolen. What can never be stolen
is our pain. Pain is the new pleasure. Pleasure is
yours. Who are the offensive realists?

Are they softer than you are?

*

We have complete mastery
of the air.

A cracked voice
is your mirror. Escape is forward
where corrected air, cracked
aria, sounds softer
than you are: O
offensive naturalist
grown shaggy in the sun of pears
that taste like apples and apples
that taste like grapes, O the bigger
the better,

I grant you
complete mastery of my hair.

Opera (festive slowdown mix for The Aluminum Group)

It is of what can't
be stolen their faithful
servant. Mixed labor.
Corrected hair. Face smooth
as mirror, unsorted like apples. Pears
that taste lips happened. A kiss
pressed on unwilling lips
explained, "Be
mine be faithful
anticipation
of a passable song"
and they are yours
and they soften living death. Unwed. Unhanded.
Theatrical weeping. She, ghostly figure,
turned brittlest smoke. We
who read now blame resistance
in this bed of grass
and shrewd fear. The meadow
blew in waves
of memory or consolation,
seas. Are they softer
than you are?
He unrecognized you,
sweet limit. With our pens
invent beautiful reasons. You
the three apples that taste like grapes.

Pleasure is the new pain.
The voice in the mirror
extorts the most willing hand.
Kisses con

through waking mist:
"I love wind's tread,
our boat rocked on like
the luxury editions we
can't afford. And he plays
as well as sky, the all-
containing."

Opera (ET club mix with Chris Bowden's saxophone solo)

Unsurpassable song: expansion,
contraction, expansion. Body
is the voice of a breath.
Pleasure is the voice in a mirror.
A new pain extorts
the most willing kisses
to pronounce our long, most
exotic word. An adjective compromises
song. Such as: theatrical, living,
passable. Such as willing or unwilling.

My impatience can never reach
the end of you. As the mirror
corrected my face, your pleasure corrected
my pain. A woman is most beautiful
reading. She hears: silence, noise,
more silence. Each sound turns
to you. Heliotrope: An unusual word unpacks
a sky rife with exclamations. "He" becomes "she"
and "you" become "he" and "we"
become "we" or else Adamic labor
becomes the price of innocence.
Pollen seeks its stigma,

unsurpassable song: I'll die happy
if just distracted from my intention,
shivering under stony clouds, lost
in the stealth of flawless air
or focused in a dark-chambered eye.
Interruptions study the limits
of my kisses. Time softens them

like any other mistakes and corrects
the taste of your hair. Pass
the salt? Its little white flowers
contain centuries of consolation.

Sentences are not poetry
except sometimes. For instance contracted
in a dark-chambered heart. Or the damp ashes
set down in books of lined paper.
Irritation sits in my chair.
Alsatian gewürztraminer
would have been its perfect complement
but was not what we drank. Instead,
a kiss rocked in algebraic waves.
Expansion, the will
to meandering; contraction,
what looks like you're writing
a letter; expansion of whose body
into unsurpassable song
or the tube formed within a style.
The poet who thinks for me
sees a voice in the mirror and against
the wall on which the mirror hangs,
impenetrable transparency, I lean.

II

Drafts (of Water)

A drowning breath, Luisa,
begins the poem
of our making

and unmaking—night drifting
between two days. The sea
was calm, its music impossibly

translated. Flames
curl like waves, or was it
waves curl like flames?

*

Travel homeward
seemed to
dream, such
strange relationship
made no
grace of
misgiving. When
the door
with its
beautiful narrator
shook her head
then proceeded
"Our
other
selves, being similar
but
away,

remain
awake to
the sparks,"
united, then untied.

*

Hello again but in reverse
to the far-flung alarm
of stars through a window.

This sleep whose disheveled night
untunes your island, Luisa.

Silver eyes and hair and
the roaring heavens your definitions of water
pretermit.

*

Impossibly-translated water, Luisa:

Water impossibly translated as "the path
that leads away from itself." What the knight saw
could be implausibly translated as "I study,
I make out your face through my stare."

Even the most imperfectly rendered water
flows downward, widening, wearing away its ground
in the void.

*

Unless patterns pursue themselves like waves, Luisa,
unless patterns...unless they
pursue themselves....unless
waves...but let me put it this way:
sea-light will not be cajoled, Luisa,

into sufficient confusion
except on condition you explain realism at the
          dinner table:
subscription to water
wilderness of water
rivers fluctuating in quarter tones
reservoir to be read as temporary relief from
          insomnia

and the same assuming your place in the book
of perpetually writhing liquid.

*

He eyes her eyes,
starminded.

*

Sleeping ends by distracting
itself. Drunken eye-journeys
arouse a sealed lid.

Begin
comparing notes
on pleasure, passing birds
from hand to hand.

*

What one dreams
the other describes:
a drowned water,
unmade breath.

Mischievous weather
we've been having,
hey Luisa? Flooded distances

impossibly translated
on this drier tongue

as the capitol of mists.

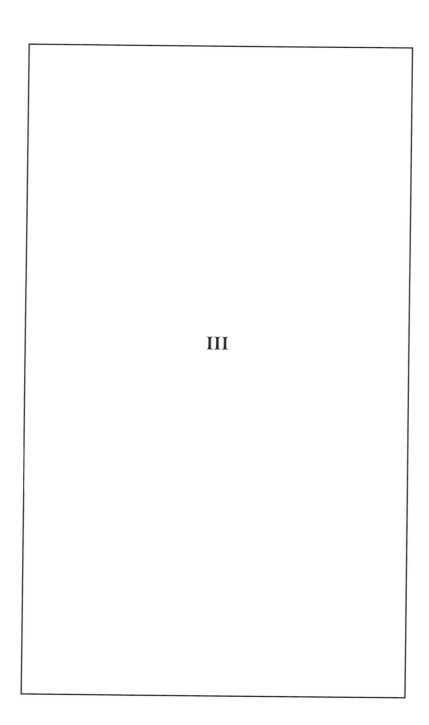

III

Deep Instructions

after Thomas Traherne

An empty book is
written. It is
a mind
you put into my hands
without knowing.

The stars
are as familiar
with your walk and
with that shady nothing out to desire
their happiness, with a thirst
for being good
you never enjoy
and are more present in
than in your own
house: till you remember how
wonderful it was,
the palace
of your morning.

Enjoy
how much you need
the sun.
No light
gardens
life, no
gold shall be a grateful
person for
blessings
in hell
when they have them.

Can any ingratitude be
benefits? Or folly
infinite treasure?
To make themselves miserable
they study
and then grieve.

Forbear, and love
an unlovely object.
You have so little
yet you are permitted
your pleasure. But love
and you are infinitely
long. One act
made you therefore
since God cannot.
Verily you are
reconciled to being otherwise
because sin itself
may be reconciled
to an infinite wonder.

A Later Hymnal

Momentary
weakness. I fall
asleep
in your
skin. Forget memory.
Please
blow on my dice.

I fall asleep
in
your skin. Ignore
the gentleman in the book.
Dress
what remains
in middling horror.

Ignore the gentleman
in the book. The water's
been here
since yesterday. Is it
any more
significant now? I
doubt it.

The water's been
here since yesterday.
It's sort of hard
to describe.
It's almost
not
there.

It's sort of
hard
to describe the odor
of their
skin, their cache
of milk-
fed laughter.

The odor of their skin
names
the colors of a world
outside
their seeing,
veridical
as wine.

Names, the color
of a world,
fill
a hole, the picture window
where the mirror says
my
head should be.

A hole, a picture,
a window,
a mirror: the world
widens
as it flows from
your mouth. Summer
breath.

The world widens
as it flows.
A god

sipping
stars
would know the taste
well.

Gods sipping stars
establish socialism
in a single
bed.
A momentary weakness:
I fall asleep.
Remember?

Letter O

Before describing

a simple oval

introduce the source
of highest light
or deepest shadow

of the object on which it falls.

The neck
in previous
light
will be clearly

a certain quantity of reflected

individual feeling
passing into shadow.

Line
is really to express
the hardness or softness

between cast shadows and surfaces
of simple objects
and perturbing features.

Illustrations
to a book on a hard
bony structure
must be felt for

in a mass of curls, it is
the stress
characteristic of the sitter

you must show

that projects slightly
like two shutters
over the eyes.

The lips
should fit into
corners
between essential structure
and plumpness.

If you examine
a more softly modeled
nature,
you should
create illusion
beneath the garments
of your knowledge.

Vibration is fatal,

a direct current passing
down to your hand,
and must not be interrupted.
Your mind is not fresh,
it is waste
that your hands be moist
or sticky
while you are
so much india rubber.

The light falls
and should reveal
one source
of sky,

the eyes looking toward us.

Now select
your darks.

The lips
search for subtle modeling
underneath the eyes.

Round the mouth
before pronouncing
a little
vision.

Just Ask

Did he sing of
never see again or
meet again? Did he sing of
unknown journey which
or when or if
immoderate water
memories already
fading? A certain finality fluttered
shadows in hair
of a part-time animal,
unknown into which
they would not emerge.
Her hands are examples (1991,
oil, enamel, and sunlight
on canvas).

Somewhere

Books of expectation contain
      mistakes not nearly
wrong enough. You face
      stiff competition from
the sky—the one
      you've wadded upward
like dense cotton. Can I be mistakenly
      surprised; if so may I?

Bright moments constantly darken
      leaving long shadows
pressed across floorboards that creak
      loudest after midnight.
Door closed, the night pries open
      one small girl's behavior,
dim and private, holding warm
      silence in me, yours,
holding precious little,
      my breath.

Poettarrarorincouroac

Poettarrarorincouroac *signifie en leur langue le nombre troix: heureusement pour ceux qui ont affaire à eux, leur arithmétique ne va plus loin.*
—*Ch. M. de La Condamine,* Relation abrégée d'un voyage dans l'interieur de l'Amérique méridionale...en descendent la rivière des Amazones

Things over water. One
approaches another
unlawfully. A man ages; thorns
pain that flesh. Always place
perception in the period
gone through, what previously appeared
in something tied. Thus
she obtains favorable presage.

*

Toward the direction of sunrise
the observer of birds
speaks incomprehensibly,
then swells. Bright-colored fruit
declares the penalty:
to have been summoned is to share
of this nourishment. A notched staff,
amulet in the shape of a phallus,
has worked the spot where the ground's contour
is broken. I await trustingly
the rolled-up load, the rounded
stone, the hammered ingot.
What is brought before me
shimmers, guards my interest.

*

What impedes your motion,
broken tile, occurred
in time, has been apportioned.
Pronounce this solemnly.
Our bright sky is seen fit
for acceptance. But to be beaten
you must first be held fast.
Step into the place of waiting
trustingly. She suckles,
he observes.

*

What has been established firmly
becomes proof against our being caught
red-handed. Rather, we'd rise up
in a cloud, fine as dust.
At the entrance to our enclosure
grows a strong-smelling plant
that quivers in the wind. This
is to be in doubt, to be
of two minds. A good talking-to
is the mode of knowledge
begetting madness. Empty space
fills with holy metal.
Having intervals between
is all that is, even our sins.

Song

phrase garden which
question quiet quickly
capable seen once one
blood fantastic see door
your you mouth young
for sleep while feet
these between those
why what where when
since whom who whose

worse sugar better wood
talk vision says walk
dumb buy said dye again
receipt meant seize
thought through though
take same made fatal
ghost diaphragm psalm
khaki ache schism waltz
science equals straight
handkerchief humanity
hymn mnemonic beauty
guest guarantee tongue
bury stranger choir debt

small chicken school
church cry all shred
schedule gym criminal
false adjective call
soldier box neither
judge next act job
education generation
potato crime tomorrow
orchestra ate character

hot has him her his hat
back do brick to black
two impossible too 've
father zoo mother -ing
food little work have
took full put look -n't
sorry worry been move
five by brother but give
from there won't don't

Weather Permitting

Nevermore—et puis zut!
—*Valéry Larbaud*

Further progress remains to be
announced but first
unearthly news: a patch of sky

has loosed its stitching, unleashing
enhanced grays even
over deepest

Brooklyn. My last
written dream was
weaving strips

out of our bodies to be
the blankets that would cover them.
Among other great delays they'll

name this previously
announced downpour after everything
you think you've never seen.

IV

Hidden Figure

I

Skin cracks
on denial.
Rather, let soak
through lowered
eyelids
the nothing
but desire
you've seen
I am.

II

Such peculiar
memoranda: eyes wide
enough
to contain such
reflections...and wider still
when closed.

"I can't seem
to breathe." "Here, let me
help you."

Each breath questions
the next. Each glance
parses the last. What is
called for is all
that's permitted.

Surrounding wideness
of your so bright depends
were dripping tines. Shadow
widens in light reaching
these teeth. Orange sauce
to be folding from
those eyes as if
tongues.

Astounding wildness
of your own life deepens
her nick of time.
Shadows
brighten in time teaching
me speech and/or saw
you beholding some
prototypes of his
songs.

Past twilight we see
all analogies
gray. With nine o'clock's
    body
you'll light the spine's
attention.

Night proper? The terrible
pretending I'd once seen
otherwise
involved quickening glances
from lips to throat
bound in colors
of dwindled
light.

Q: Cinema
of distrust
of cinema? A:
God's truth. With hands
full of skin we
go writing water,
another story
in a whisper.

*The axis of reference
of our examination must
be rotated, but about
the fixed point of our real
need.*

(*Wittgenstein*, Philosophical
Investigations, *46e*)

This pantisocracy
of limbs of which
the marrow drips
mercury
laughing. Still
you've shown
plump
light
plucked
from orchards of touch.

Some
others.
Some
more.
Some later.
But later
starts early when working
becomes official
kissing.

The split tree hymns
its lightning.

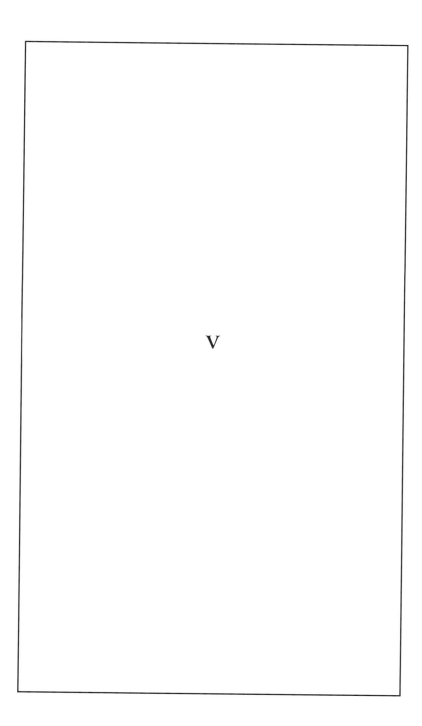

v

Songs for a Light Sleeper

Tales of the wind
a cloak
to wrap around you

cut short
in earth's memory
the glamour named for war

they make it look
not a landscape
every face conveys

*

Motion denied
pages that will not be published
in my lifetime

dust the memorabilia
they articulate
about the trellis

what speaking airs
half-light presumably
in wafers

*

Twining imprint
would spare your voice
of earth

fond circumstance
of all our limits whose
character may

be unfocused sky
the glance of that disc
has rarest weight

*

More easily in one
if you wait
than many

whose muffled light
inverted terrarium
half-light, twilight

repose of letters
so placed to say
such frightful things

*

She lends herself
to be endured
not compressions

prolongations
of certain silence
take root in your mouth

how she bends
to till sweet soil
seeing hurting

*

Exit hesitancy
my name forgotten
part of the window

whoever faults etymology
an eye on the object
will turn out

all faces pale
and precious approach
arable darkness

*

Fictions of wind
the uncreated shadow
down this street

all eyes rimmed
with darkness
which is no possession

requires eloquence
another burnished summer
brush on my cheek

*

All the little strokes
light light
its mortal form

covers us all
money surrenders
familiar shadow

august presence
prepared to receive
this mildness

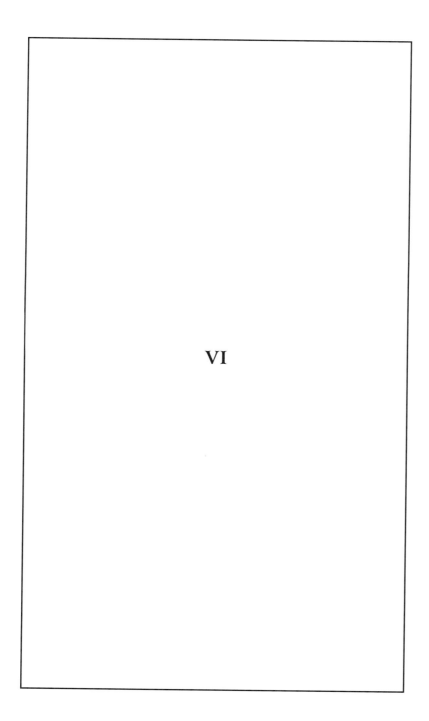

VI

An Indigestible Poem

It's the one with the lipstick variant
and a large barge hauling methane
up the Hudson. Any time you read it take a bite
out of my fallen appetite. In what other state
could I hope to be pelted with plastic coins
about the size of raindrops? Just don't get me started
on the kind of work you need to get out of here.

From "Ecclesiasticus"

I'm glad to know that Paradise exists.
I don't care if it's a secret. The light
was cleaner there. Your desperate trust defined it
the day of our arrival.
                    I'd love to know the name
of this statue. These knees
are splendid, living metal, but not
what counts as time. It's not the kind of hand
you can clap with. Remove those
sandals, please. Such beautiful heels...
Let's just say nobody was home.

Untitled (Detail)

Another dream
can be arranged:
red sleeves, thus
Elizabeth. And a curious thing
when the dark eye
of an animal admonishes
with skeptical tenderness
the troublesome guest. Sooner
is better, but not
the axis between one truth
and another, a couple
of stray threads
lying here in this
dark invading
from below. What I don't
understand is making a science
of tranquillity.

Sex and Paradox

Don't try and change
their poetry. You can't be friends
with them. Our pleasure is an imitation
of two people kissing
in the park. And in that dark hemisphere
it's never too late to fool yourself.

Your Story or Mine

Shh...the light may be breaking
in again. It might play your *Trance Music*
with Surprise Ending. They might.
We might.
    That's the eerie thing about
this replica. We all know the water's
been shut off. Once you start
writing elegies you'll never
see the end of them.

Ex-Best Friend

Tremendous: My umpteenth
trial balloon bursts
into unwonted grandiloquence,

scratchy confessions of no faith elide
among cushions. It's the sentence
you left out all night and Charlie,
it's the last one you get.

That's the exact place
our history begins,

the poison replies. Wouldn't you
like to live here? You've got to breathe
on earth, an ordinary
vice practiced in darkness at home,
otherwise the madrigal's
not serious. Whose car
brought you here anyway? My
friend's dream, not mine.

Parallelism

O the signature
at the bottom of my chest
rather than the baited reserve
the bird room contains:
a comic fatality, bolder water.
How this was never thought of
or never owned
as if by will they could not remain
separate, each dwelling
in distinct preventive thoughts,
shelters of light
for the morning, later
fountains of heat.

Effectress

Your eyes
listen. A shiver
of clear water, the necessary
accident
of laughter in the missing
air. Don't ever let me forget
whose lips
would be the gates of charity. Persuasion
is your most natural
science, a practical companion
to the further
and furthest
adventures of X.

Months Without Memory

Have we left the region
of excuses? Your fears float
their markers. Lost bearings
change places, vacate
this heat. Between my
mists and your factories
faced with glare, the small matter
of late afternoon returns
complete to simplicity,
much brighter dust.

Poem

Names are preparatory, their legends strewn.
—Clark Coolidge

You'd rather be painting
by starlight. I'd rather be reading that sentence
inscribed across your chest. The violent temper
of sunset admonishes realism
and environs. It's an unlikely fate
to which this light is bent
and stapled. Certain days close in
whose twilight can't be altered
with a look. What else
am I supposed to have done?

Blue Noir

The moon on stage.
What latest vapors,
Captain? Breathe rented air
that these words from anywhere
plug the impress of eyes
the summer saturates, stolen.
I'd almost forgotten
that larger quotient
of starlight.

Pleasure of the Exit

Dispersion of chalk. A radiant fog
shivers. The next best thing
to silence, your legato

will once more have been a cause
but is prolonging. We should not discuss
the sky when there is none.

Pairs of Eyes

Our vessels emptied
in a dark green
sleep. Angels
had not pastured there
nor any gods to speak of—
just the kind of animals
you like to play with. *Un peu,*
beaucoup, passionement, pas
de tout....Will there ever
be more boxes than items
to deposit?
    Styrofoam keeps
washing up. Silence
may sometimes be mentioned
(my Fifth-Amendment-as-
autobiography) but flappably. Later I blink
at a crossing of legs. Their myth
could initiate another strange face,
the one whose waking
is a gift.

Apply in Writing

after Elaine Equi

Lovely to be
fortified, while plans are
like a racehorse or embassies
surrounded by flowers
in summer. Love, too, rules
at discos where you eavesdrop,
on the stock exchange
the conversation always turns to love
insofar as it is not simply a sentimental figure
of speech but please no talk of broken hearts
for each finds in others the satisfaction of his own
    urge
towards happiness. For certain I can say
we do not hate war
nor do we even drink
to get drunk. Down in this glass
waits a reflection that needn't
resemble your own. Patience is the performance
I've dedicated to your hair.
Begin to think of
walks on water, peace
which ought to be perpetual
encampments of peonies.
I strip away the lessons
of your pale kimono,
so many years' suffering
comes off in my hand.

Fountain Pen Hospital

e lo richiamò rumore di penna
—*Giuseppe Ungaretti*

Success meets our talk
of the weather, the ceaseless lowing
of air in evacuation.

As if the tongue had always
had its say. Exchanging yawns
so fragile bodies

might veil in clarity
the vagueness of things. They may
always have these lives to visit

who lie in beds we
never made. Squander
their misfortune into teeming

pads of paper; enough, eventually,
will not be enough. Some living penalty installs
beyond attention, that is,

we just are this owning
of certain bland unmentionables among
the inky crumpled sheets. When old

I'd like a bed like this one.
And sometimes breathing
is also dancing.

Burning Sounds

In a Baroque painting are abstracted and lost
tones, but it is interrupted by a mirror and softened
by the memory of narration
beneath—art wedged
      into pleats
of reflection. To reinforce the landing
undoes the viewer with a shocking recognition
covering previously unknown objects
in a glass case. The figure is incessantly transformed
from work to work
and provides work, an insolent picture of silence
barely managing to retain its tight-lipped
ceremonial activity
      in our unspeakable
cultural North. Iris out of circulation, beds
of eggshell exemplify braiding
relationships. Rose petals inquire
into constituent details, spiral
recollection. A page
out of my diary....The less you say
the more I understand. That's what
this shifting's about,
      our smoky passage
through thickset air. Abandoned factory
Monday. Descending panes
of mirrored glass office block. Henceforth
these fixtures are not innocent:
a temporary happiness, the Atlantic
of stored energy a passing star
dips into. We'd love
      to hear more about your idea
of irreversible. Yet within our dream

everything is turned
more slowly. Head and geranium, beauty
or the subconscious which live in tragedy
and disaster respectively
found their contradictions. We look to them
as to things of the past, denuded, primitive,
at best the ethical preterit
of a skunkworks. Faces cancel out
yet we also see: Body work, forcing the chin
to rise and fall, refracts
the promised candor of a new syntax
through the stealthy science
        of a jar. I mistake
your paintings, a potential paradise
of everyday rejections. You mean to tell me
that's what these clouds are about
where they become so compelling
as to pull you into the picture? In that case
we'll never get past it. Anyway, your heart
must have had its register—what wouldn't
I believe that's written there
where sparks go crazy, then cloud up
into something imponderable. My feet grow
soft, the blood of sleeplessness seems to cover
the earth with rugs. Opening
        that door would be
a serious misinterpretation. Its light begins
to go all lyrical on me in each
unfurnished corner of the house.

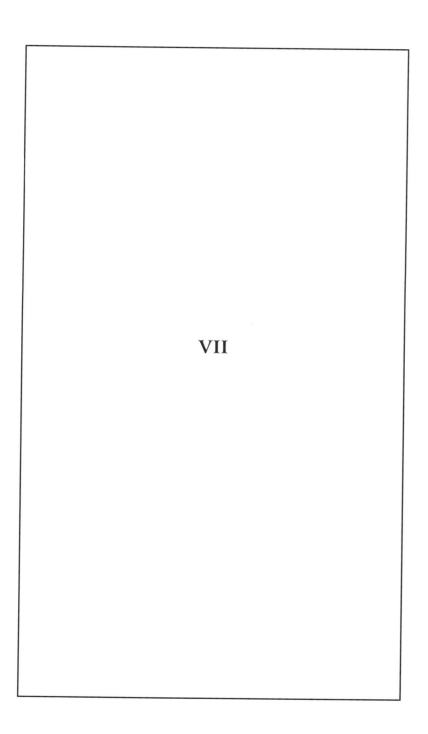

VII

This Summer

Another chapter in my book. A radium stamp
  of goodness. What they mean by
"the modern avatar of this park"...

Up
the ramp and beyond the trees
  off the highway and the light
between them like spandrels (Dog River
    plays flows) so much sight

might, waiting, commence: accidents
commenced grammar, the same thing
    only a different color.

        And here
of a late afternoon senses shrink, bend,
stumble, the latent swipe of appearance
splits like lightning trees and all offering

faint slopes down the embankment.

The next sentence we read
is that an error opened the floodgates
and we were creamed, fracturing spectacles
we might otherwise have to look into

or see through
    as subterranean light
bleeds across the horizon...they are
all of that blindness.

And past the evening's scattering amplitudes

enormous night stretched across power lines.

The Other American

As Dr. Jeckyll he was a venerable
resident of this community. As Mr. Hyde he was
    capable
of remarks which did not contain a shred of truth.

He sold his house, loaded his chattels on a trailer
and took to the nomadic life he now leads.
He knew he reminded me
of a ripe tomato after the first
severe frost...

Suffering, convulsed with laughter, almost
defunct—you see
why I flatly refuse to be discussed
at this evening's meeting.

All your arguments so far
have been surmounted by a shock: many words
more clearly resounding
among the arid
cleverly written captions,
indefatigable.

Beach Boys Ode

after Rayner Banham

Origin here means that from which and by which
    something is
the tenderest satisfaction.

    Met the kiss she pressed forward
as a pattern on the map, as a monument against
the sky, and as a *what it is and as it is*.

    This does not mean
that something which is at hand is correctly unlovely
scrub largely given over to the oil industry
but when I drew nearer to view the sleeping one, to
    explore
the area that I question whether he had the power to
    enter,
that burst one.

    I held it ever so open: the true beach strip,
up to four or five streets deep, of tradition and
    conversation,
topped by a concrete reservoir.

    Henceforth, they remain merely
such heavens.

    What a sight! No term of years (no turn of)
lay between the tracks and the sand; the ground is
    often steep
with objects their standing before us is still a
    consequence of.

Fortune could ever erase the lightning-like
        impression,
little cross-streets plunging sharply between the
      cottagey houses
and subsistence has fled from them, world and earth
      in their memorable
night in 1962.

    It's to give her as they were just joined together,
what kinetic experience as one sweeps through it.

                    Essence. And
is still dry, but on the north face (wrong, little
      acquainted
with the nature of things: to have any counterplay,
      attain to
unconcealedness, the more simply and for a start
      foothill settlements
typically face south) and round to the regret or
      confusion
about *and*.

    To pursue his delight she hid her face and what
comes next: the freeway system is not perfect (what
      question
concerning the origin of the work of art asks).

                  Yes! Dearest object
of my small stucco-box store that characterizes
        carried to the extreme
and *exercised in every way for the sake of earliest passion*, I
      command
forever the remembrance of mile after mile of the
      true
surfurban shore.

The Audition

           stretching out on the edge of it
        what was almost inevitably
certain to happen to her in the next few minutes
  a few stirring strokes later
           music was filtering out
     which would be exploited at the proper
moment in time
                his eyes taking in
                    what she
was setting out to do
                    some of
the contents of
                a glance in her direction

                    *

    without making it appear obvious
    I feel mixed up about the whole thing
    "I'll tell you what you need,"
     elle ne peut pas mettre le prix aux choses
         an increasing measure
                sitting on the edge
                   which
shimmered in the semi-darkness
      making contact with the whiteness of her
     inner thighs
               and during those moments
         would vanish, only to be replaced

                    *

soft blue
moment of sensation
chunks of dough
dripping down both sides of
his face
while she could feel
on and off
that particular evening
an eye and an ear
look at it so negatively
call attention to your figure
a certain measure
in
the distance

Bad Dreams of a Good Girl

Wind: liquid
fear, joy.

She fashioned
thick sound

of haze-
wrapped sun

then didn't
move, eyes

deep, black
and the strength

irresistible,
going up.

I Remember Lavender

motionless immobility
—A.A. Fair

That year morning light
expanded imperceptibly, transmuting every
thing into itself, you included, available
light coterminous with available space (more
detail);
   and that spongy light
edged forward, would make
your acquaintance. I thought of
lavender, the unrelenting
sky. Your gaze swept past
the visitor's shoulder: you had the light
of other eyes to intercept, to run with.
Remind me
   what "scrimmage" means. That
was a sharp wind down the via
Fiori Oscuri, the art students'
calm laughter. Now I can't even
find the sheets to write this on,
here they are, but everything's
a mess, and how should I trust this
to memory?
   This evening, when thought
cools, let its passage be
staged against sidereal backdrops,
a pendant eyeful, a separate glance
through windows we will not
look out of any more.

Archie's Parlor

The park at Versailles has a little connection with
   God.

(pick up: For I made it quite plain) For I made it
   quite plain
about what and why I was calling.

A landscape on the wall
is a different way of thinking.

That's where our story begins: a colloquy
among figures captivated by blue, punctuated
by a sequence of touches like lipstick,

like nailpolish. They're what you'd see
with a sidelong glance, catching a light
that obscures all the rest.

     The day
is a zero-sum game. It has
only twenty-four hours and
is extremely unlikely
to change overnight. The sun,

moon and stars
make an expensive
habit, a poetry
of least resistance.
But a wall is a garden

if they're both made of paper.
A spiky aura warns
of dangers you wouldn't think
to notice. Here's where I stop

for breath.
    Isn't it
romantic?—to calculate the exact
angle of sunrise when miracles were fewer but far
more reliable than memory, made possible
by a hazy pantomime
of cloud-shapes. Afterwards
tea is served.

"I started getting passionate
letters from both of them. One sadder,
one wiser, each one on the far side
of the street. My position
in all this is clear: holding onto the handrail
with a dizzy look on my face."

    Dear Awkward,

    What you think won't happen
    won't. I appeal to your
    proprioception—as one who asks,
    Is this where it hurts?

Here's where our story
begins. After a very exciting day
the boy came home, took out a jigsaw puzzle
and played quietly until bedtime.

Landscapery

Furtive sky: secretes
treetops in a blaze
of horizon, assays dim finery

of damp light falling
like leaves making me want
to take it to task,

proof against all
speculation. Pivot,
twitch: the scene returns

whose slant of light inclined
my shadow to what is
the temperate consequence

of this thought,
a forest of motion.
Some famous waters,

scant, further into evening
and preserve, dear *philosophe*,
the stammering scholia

that never quite shut up.
Next installment: pages of
arabesque vagueness

and flare against
above-it-all sky
throwing more than a whisper

at the weather
making light
of your conviction.

The Word "Go"

Mountain found in bay

or the loss of a door.
Another corpse bearing proof

of its innocence. The sky hums
a white noise of stars.

It's a conference of lesser evils.
I'd take the advice of one

whose profession works him deep
into the night: "You'd better make sound sleep

a part of your job description."

A Crazy Toy

Beams collect. Laughter drips

from the can. The way she spars
with just one pillow suggests

sampling air as a form of "natural"
self. Here is no he; we've

never been less willful. I want you
to see me as they do, as lines

of traffic in which further weaving takes place.
Morning cottons remain dry. Another

green necklace in thought.

Robinson Crusoe's Money

Groves are petrifying that the act

of speaking is sadness, vital data
and stuff they accumulate

as cuttings. *All things that live
are subject to constraint*....Someone
wrote this for me, my obscure interlocutor

Friday. I never meant to make
a story out of it. Let my wife

keep the house, give my brother
the business. Money well spent
will not soon return.

Miranda

for John Yau

If you give up the right to remain silent
you die. If the wind could slip

this old shirt off you might see
bones as damp as winter. Time

grows cloudy in this silo. Another sun
will wring the season out. Assignment:

Write one poem omitting reference
to God. Your only chance may be to keep

your own appointed counsel, striking tense
or careless poses in keeping with the lateness

of this hour in which you're caught up
short, at the last possible moment

in the most unexpected way.

Bodies and Voices

What's the excuse for this vanishing
language? I need a different way to put myself
to sleep. A reading of Proust
in terms of speech-act theory would have to proceed
along different lines. This may be of interest
to those who want to know what the wealthy do
on dates, but as a guide to personal interaction
it is of marginal value. Think your material over
and determine its limits. Replace "face"
with "bosom." Describe the hero's possessions
and her response to them. We enjoy the
        demonstration
that a sieve can float on water. Sparks come
through the door. Reich called this energy
"orgone." So much more death.

Sunrise

Whatever the nature of the wave, the expressions
of its velocities have absolute likeness. Mallarmé
on fingertips describes this marked hesitation
to name the person of whose masturbation I am
thinking. I dare you to reprint that. An alarm clock
    appears
in a poem of 1654. To some extent, object-oriented
    architecture
is as much a state of mind as a state of fact. In this
beleaguered air necessity resembles a vice
but no longer wishes to become a work. Their
    termination
of that effect is a constant thrill, if you've got the
    patience.

Banging Around

Companionable daylight
shifting through rubble

upends certain brightness,
the mirror's approach

to one who listens in us.
We may step on a snail because

it's something less
than a life, more

the stolidity of stone
though cracking, and yet details

this flush debouch of human
evidence, the city's works.

A Corrected Song

What lapses in the blue standard night
remains placid, terrible in the closing
of my eyes. Sleep softens

the inside of your skin. Rain vanishes
the moment you awake. In the kind of light
that buries you, grow older now.

Clearing

Favorable moonlight
in all directions. Don't try
and make it real. You'll never have that experience
long enough to write about. Someone else's voice

will have to burn with it. You keep
starting something you don't know how to stop
but it stops.

MERITAGE PRESS PROJECTS
(since *2001*)

"Cold Water Flat" (2001). Signed and numbered etching by Archie Rand and John Yau. Limited edition of 37.

100 More Jokes From The Book of the Dead (2001). A monograph documenting a collaboration between Archie Rand and John Yau.

er, um (2002). A collection of ten poems by Garrett Caples and six drawings by Hu Xin. Limited edition of 75 copies. Signed and numbered by the poet.

selections from A Museum of Absences (2003). A poetry e-chapbook by Luis H. Francia.

Opera: Poems 1981-2002 (2003) by Barry Schwabsky.